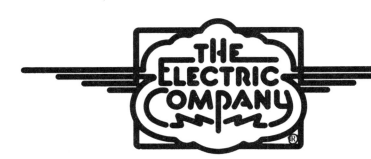

MAKE YOUR OWN MAGIC SHOW!

By Aldo Bonura
Illustrated by Loring Eutemey

Publishers · GROSSET & DUNLAP · New York
A FILMWAYS COMPANY
Children's Television Workshop · New York

ISBN: 0-448-16404-3

Table of Contents

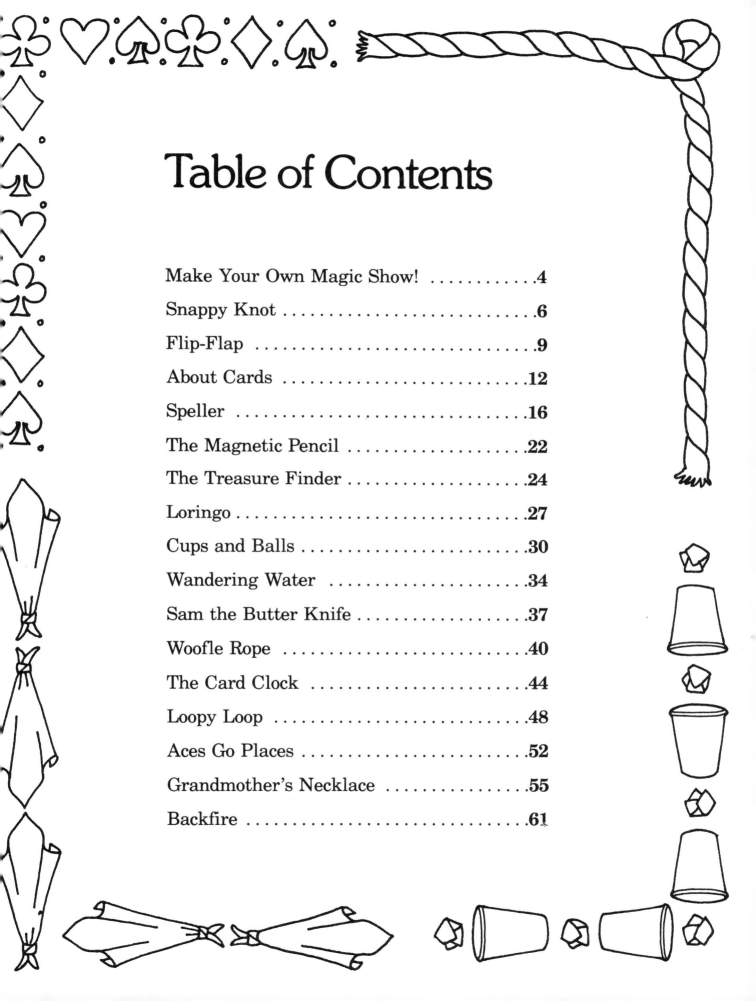

MAKE YOUR OWN MAGIC SHOW!

Here is a way to put on a magic show with things you can find. *Doing* magic is different from just knowing how a trick is done. You can find out how a trick is done just by reading it. But to *do* magic you will need the three P's—PROPS, PATTER and PRACTICE.

PROPS

are the things you need when you do a trick;

PATTER

is what you say while you are doing the trick;

PRACTICE

is doing the trick by yourself—in front of a mirror or for a good friend, if it helps you—until you think you're ready to do the trick in front of an audience.

Before you begin to practice, read the trick once from beginning to end. Then get the props you need. Now read through the trick again, step by step. Do the trick slowly, using your props. Be sure to look carefully at the pictures. Finish one step before going on to the next. Say the patter as you go along.

If you think of other things to say, something different from the patter in the book, use your own patter, but be sure to practice it. Make up your own magic words, too. But be sure you don't use the same words for different tricks. Each trick should have its own special words.

Now you're ready! Pick some tricks, put them in the order you like, get your props ready, say the patter . . . and you'll be doing a magic show! You'll need a table, and a costume—if you want to wear one.

If you can borrow some props from the audience, that's good. That will surprise them even more. When you perform magic, you will usually need an assistant—someone you ask to come up to help you. Always ask somebody in particular. Otherwise, everybody will rush up together.

So, practice with your props, follow the pictures, learn your patter, and you will be ready to MAKE YOUR OWN MAGIC SHOW!

Snappy Knot

Effect:
You snap a handkerchief.
A knot appears.

Prop:
One handkerchief.

To get ready:
Tie a knot in one corner
of a handkerchief.

6

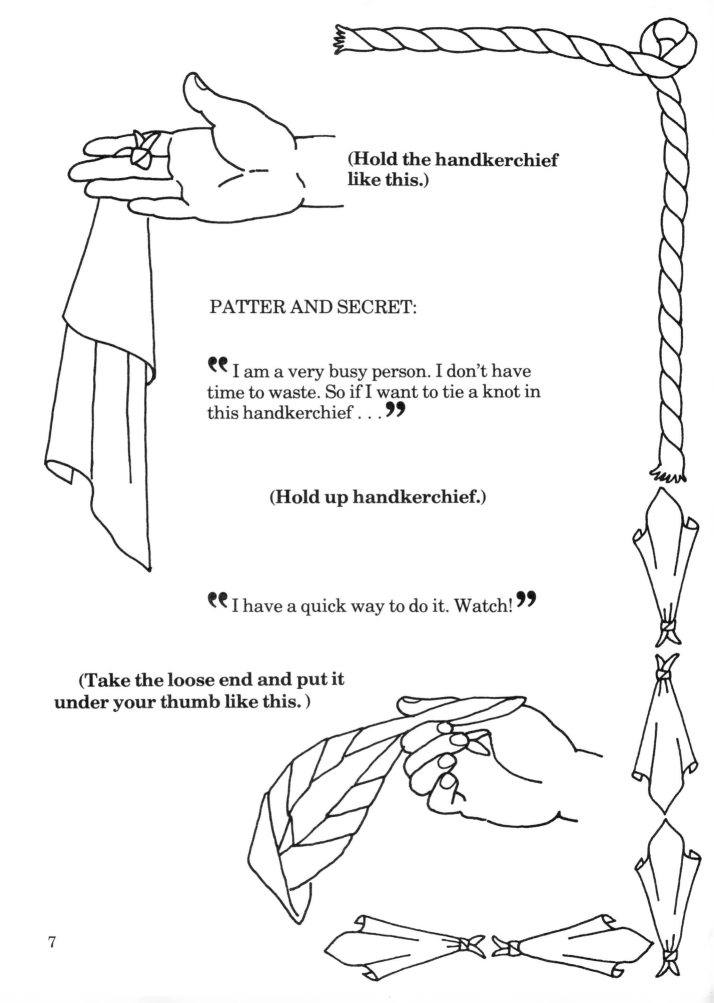

(Hold the handkerchief like this.)

PATTER AND SECRET:

❝ I am a very busy person. I don't have time to waste. So if I want to tie a knot in this handkerchief . . . ❞

(Hold up handkerchief.)

❝ I have a quick way to do it. Watch! ❞

(Take the loose end and put it under your thumb like this.)

Snap down and let that end go—but hang on to the knot.)

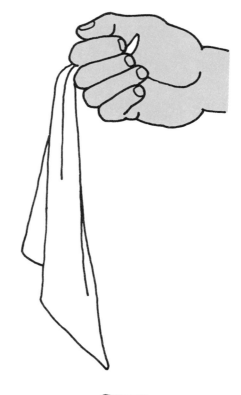

❝ I missed! Well, it doesn't work *every* time. Here—I'll try again. **❞**

(Snap again—the same way.)

❝ I don't know why it's not working. Oh, I know—I forgot the magic words. **❞**

(Snap again. But this time hold on to the end under your thumb, and let go of the knot.)

❝ Snappy Knot! **❞**

(Say these magic words as you snap. Hold the handkerchief up very high so everyone can see the knot.)

❝ There! It's a very quick way to tie a knot. Thank you. **❞**

(Bow.)

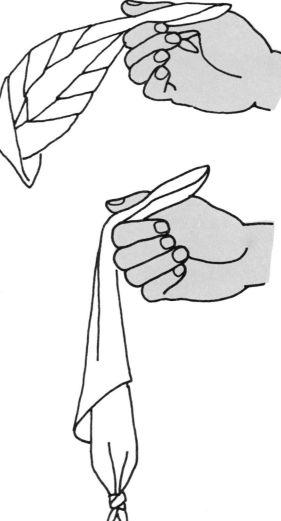

NOTE: This effect works very well with a rope, too.

NOTE AGAIN: This trick is good to do just before "Flip-Flap."

Flip-Flap

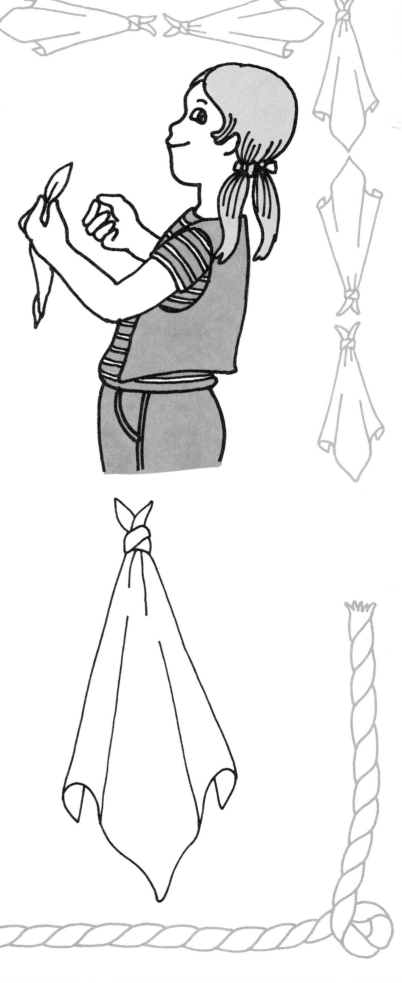

Effect:

The knot on a handkerchief moves around when you pull an invisible hair.

Prop:

One handkerchief.

PATTER AND SECRET:

You can do this trick after "Snappy Knot." If you do, say—

"Now, I'll show you why I wanted a knot in this handkerchief."

If you're not doing this trick after "Snappy Knot," start by saying—

"Please watch this handkerchief. I'm just going to tie a knot in one corner. I'll hold it up like this."

(Pull up on handkerchief to make it stand up straight.)

"Now may I borrow one of your hairs, please?"

(Reach over and pretend to pull a hair out of someone's head.)

"Thank you. Now, that didn't hurt, did it? I'll now wrap the hair around this knot."

(Pretend to do so.)

"Now watch what happens when I pull on the hair."

(One hand is pretending to pull on the hair. The hand that is holding the handkerchief secretly makes the knot move with the thumb and the first finger. See the pictures.)

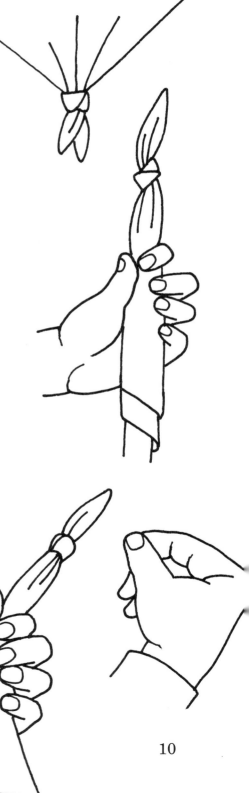

" Now watch what happens when I pull on the other side. **"**

(See the picture. You make the knot go the other way.)

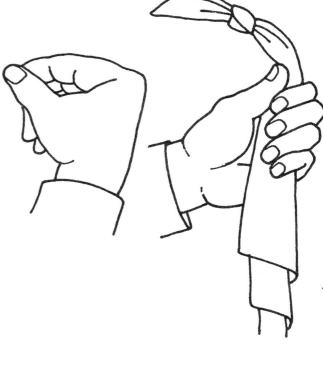

" Now I'll make it stand straight up again. That's really very easy. This is much harder. Watch. **"**

(You make the knot go the wrong way. See the picture. Do this three or four times, with the knot going the wrong way.)

" Isn't that silly? Well, it's time to stop now. **"**

(Make the knot stand straight up again. Pretend to unwind the hair from the knot.)

" Here is your hair back again. Thank you very much. **"**

(Pretend to put the hair back into the person's head.)

About Cards

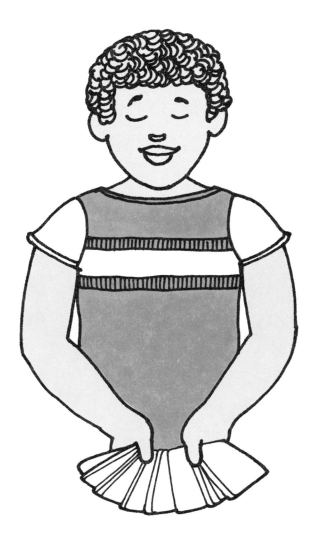

Here are some things you need to know about cards that you will be using in lots of different card tricks. These things need to be practiced, just like the tricks. Follow the pictures step by step with a deck of cards in your hands. Soon you'll begin to be a real card magician.

SHUFFLE. Hold the deck in one hand. Have the backs of the cards to the audience.

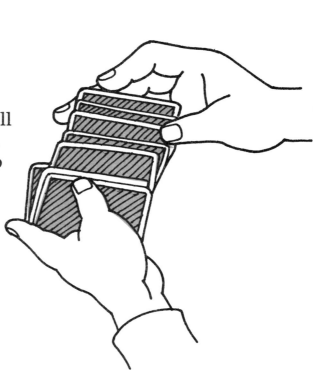

With the other hand, lift about half of the cards from the bottom.

Put that stack on the top, and pull a few cards off with your thumb. Keep doing that until you use up the stack.

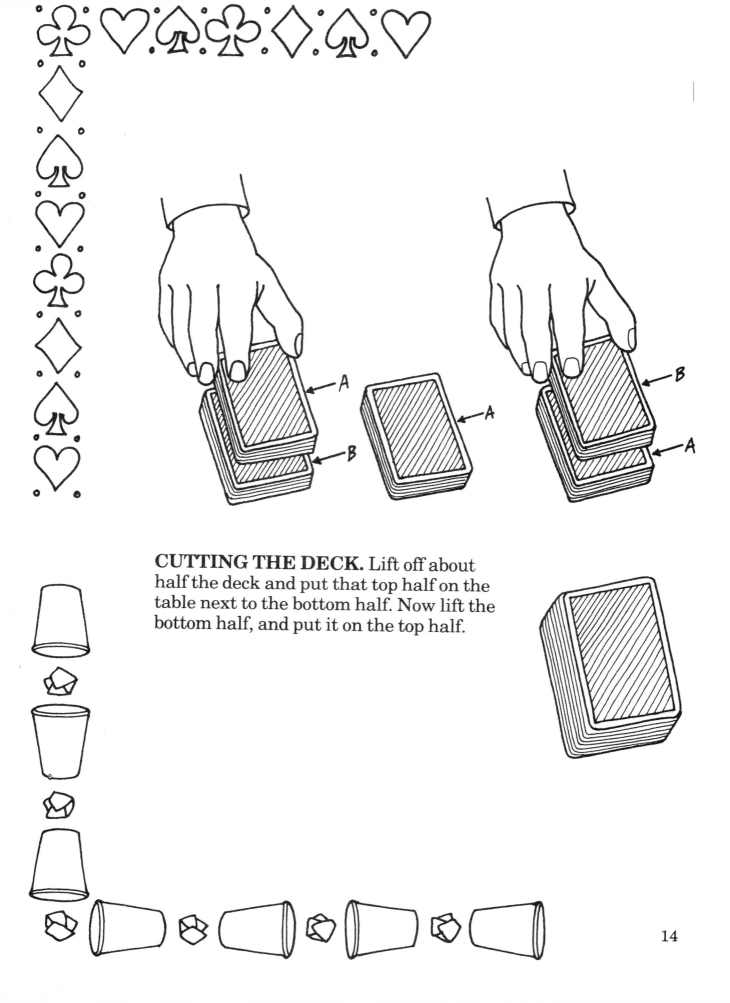

CUTTING THE DECK. Lift off about half the deck and put that top half on the table next to the bottom half. Now lift the bottom half, and put it on the top half.

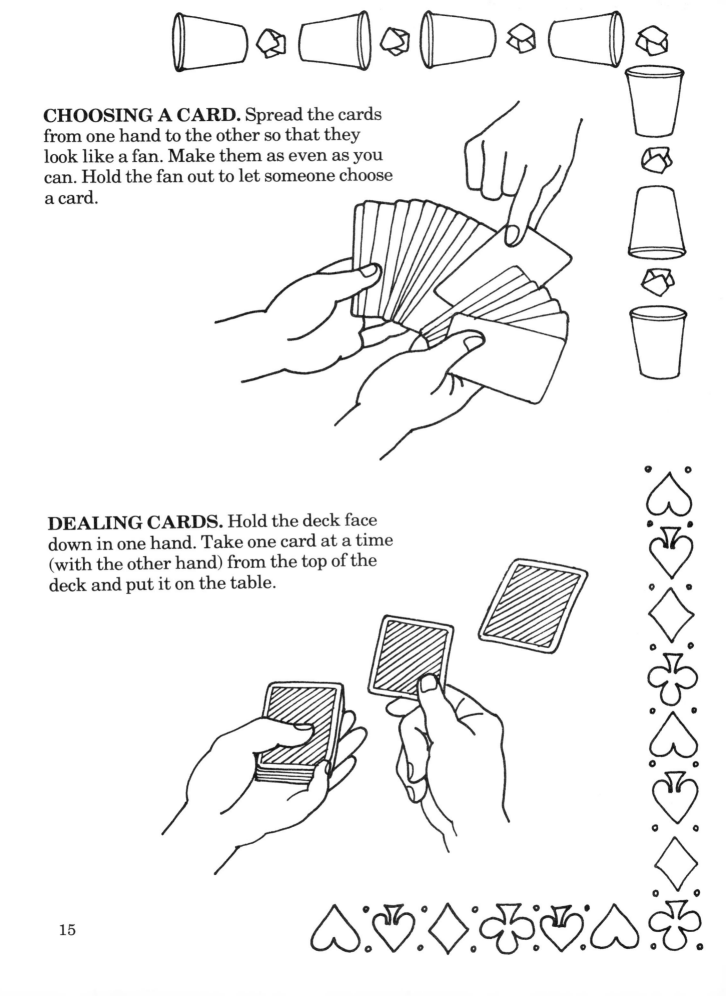

CHOOSING A CARD. Spread the cards from one hand to the other so that they look like a fan. Make them as even as you can. Hold the fan out to let someone choose a card.

DEALING CARDS. Hold the deck face down in one hand. Take one card at a time (with the other hand) from the top of the deck and put it on the table.

Speller

Effect:

You will magically produce
the Six of Spades.

Prop:

One deck of cards.

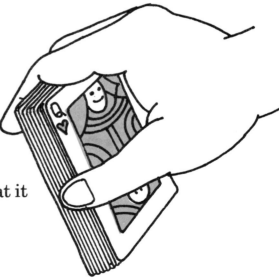

To get ready:

Be sure you know the card on
the bottom of the deck. You can peek at it
when you get the deck ready. Let's
say the bottom card is the Queen of
Hearts.

PATTER AND SECRET:

" Please take a card, any card that strikes your fancy, although we don't have any fancy cards, just playing cards! Please memorize the card. Drop your card on top of the deck. Picture the card in your mind. Please give the deck one complete cut. **"**

(Finish the cut if your friend doesn't. That makes the Queen of Hearts land next to the chosen card, which we'll say is the Six of Spades.)

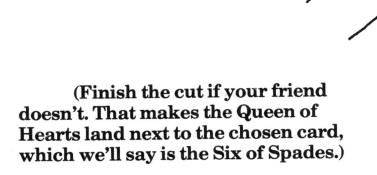

6 OF SPADES

QUEEN OF HEARTS

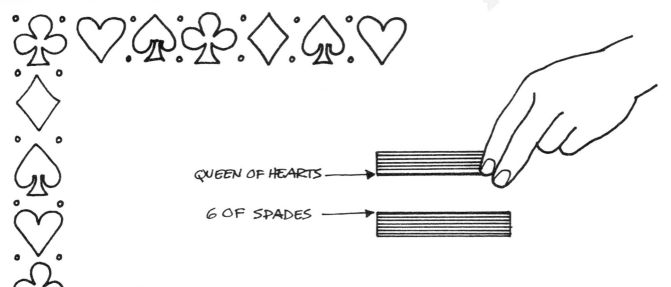

QUEEN OF HEARTS →

6 OF SPADES →

❝Say the name of the card to yourself—slowly. I now take the deck and turn it face up. As I spread the cards, be sure your card is still there. And picture it again in your mind.❞

(When you turn the deck over and go through the cards face up, you'll see the Six of Spades right on top of the Queen of Hearts.)

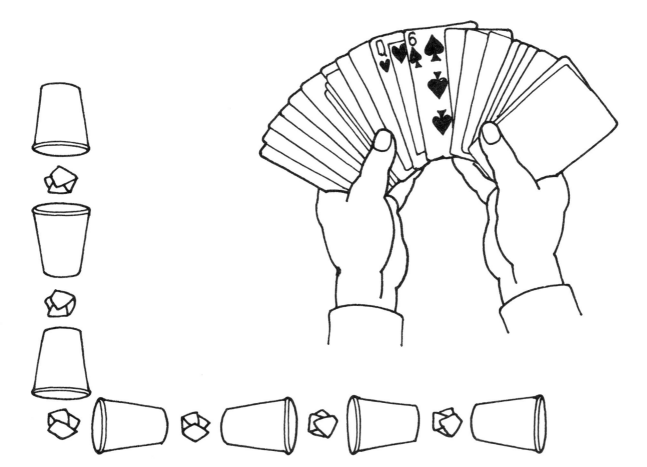

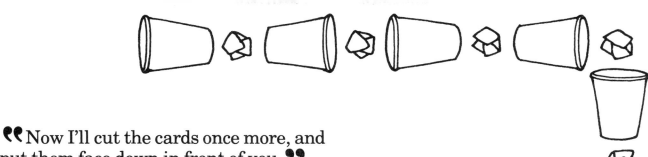

Now I'll cut the cards once more, and put them face down in front of you.

(Now hold the cards so nobody can see the faces. Cut the cards by breaking the deck between the Six of Spades and the Queen of Hearts.

When you put the two parts together face down, the Six of Spades will be on top of the deck again.)

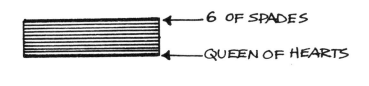

6 OF SPADES

QUEEN OF HEARTS

❝ I'm going to ask you to tell me the name of your card now, please! (For example, "The Six of Spades.") I'll just spell that ...S — I —**❞**

(Put the top card on the table face down.)

(The next card goes on top of the first. Just keep on spelling the name of the card, putting another card down for each letter.)

❝ X — O — F — S — P — A — D — E — S **❞**

(Turn this last card face up. It'll be the wrong card!)

❝Well, I missed! But why don't you try? Here, you do what I did.❞

(Turn that last card face down on top of the stack you "spelled" off the deck. Drop the stack on top of the deck and hand it to your friend.)

WRONG CARD

❝Just spell "Six of Spades," taking off one card for each letter . . .

S — I — X — O — F — S — P — A — D — E —❞

(On the last card say)

❝Now turn over that last card. S.❞

(It'll be the Six of Spades!)

❝Thank you! I knew you could do it!❞

LAST CARD

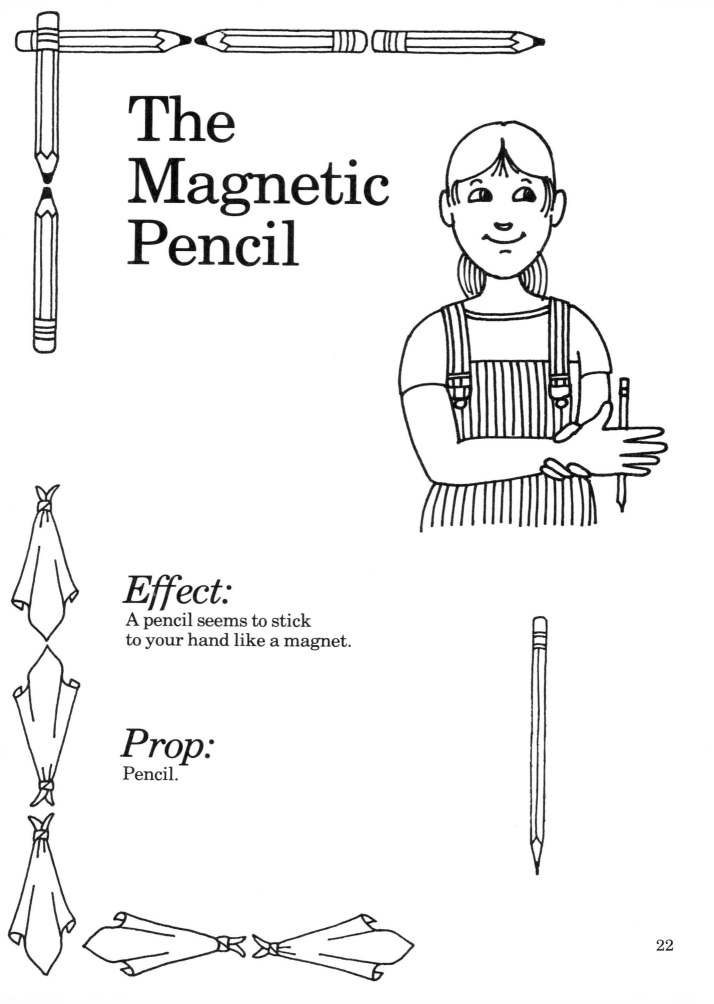

The Magnetic Pencil

Effect:
A pencil seems to stick
to your hand like a magnet.

Prop:
Pencil.

22

PATTER AND SECRET:

❝I want to show you my magnetic pencil. It's a funny kind of magnet. It sticks to my hand. Look!❞

(This is how it looks to you. Your right thumb holds the pencil. But so does your left index finger.)

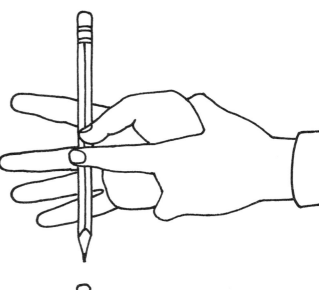

❝What's that? You want to know what happened to my thumb? Oh, you want real magic. For that, I'll have to say the magic words Cat-A-By-Clop!❞

(With this, lift your right thumb. The pencil sticks.)

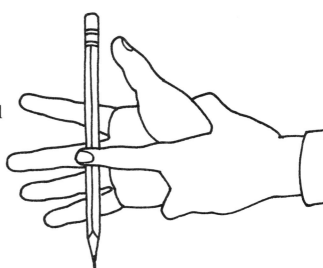

(This is what the audience sees:)

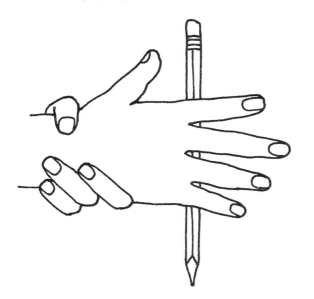

❝ And now I'll say the magic words backwards: Clop-By-A-Cat!❞

(Drop the pencil, hold up your hands showing both palms. Take a bow. Do this trick just before The Treasure Finder.)

The Treasure Finder

Effect:

With your magnetic pencil you can find a hidden coin.

(Do this effect right after The Magnetic Pencil.)

Props:

Coin (borrowed from audience)
Pencil (not borrowed)
Table

PATTER AND SECRET:

❝ I would like to borrow a coin from the audience. I promise not to spend it. A quarter would be fine. Please put the coin on the table. Now look at this pencil.❞

(Hold pencil up high so everyone can see it.)

❝ It is a magnetic pencil. Now, I'll need four assistants— you, you, you, and you! ❞

(Have all four stand by the table. If you don't have four people, two will do. But you need at least two.)

❝ I will now turn my back. While my back is turned, I'd like one of you, please, to pick up the coin, make a fist with the coin inside, and hold it up to your forehead. Don't let me know who will do this . . . I am now holding the magnetic pencil up in the air. Think very hard about the coin. Keep your hand on your forehead. Try to send a picture of the coin to my magnetic pencil. Keep doing that while I say these magic words: Boom-Ba-La-Foo-Foo–Golly-Woggy-Frazzle-Dazzle! ❞

(Say these magic words three times.)

❝Now ALL of you close both hands and EVERYBODY put both hands on the table. That's all four assistants, please. The one who is holding the coin: just keep the coin in your hand and put both hands on the table with the other assistants.❞

(Turn around and face them.)

❝Please hold your hands still. I will pass the magic pencil above all of the hands. When the pencil finds the coin, it will wiggle.❞

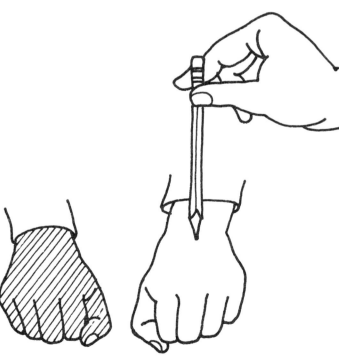

(Hold the pencil as in the picture, point down. Move it slowly above the hands while you say, "Boom-Ba-La-Foo-Foo–Golly-Woggy-Frazzle-Dazzle!" Just look for the hand that is lighter in color than that person's other hand. That hand should be paler because blood leaves a hand that is held up to the forehead. Stop over that hand and wiggle the pencil—but not before saying the magic words three times again.)

❝Look! The magnetic pencil has found something. Please open your hand. It's the coin! Please hold it up and show it to everybody. Thank you, all. Let's have a hand for all the assistants, and especially for . . .❞

(Hold up pencil)

❝. . . the marvelous magical magnetic pencil—The Treasure Finder!❞

Loringo

Loringo is the greatest magician in the town of Mule Shoe, Rhode Island. Here is his greatest trick.

Effect:

By just feeling a card you can tell what it is.

Prop:

One deck of cards.

To get ready:

Make sure there are no jokers in the deck.

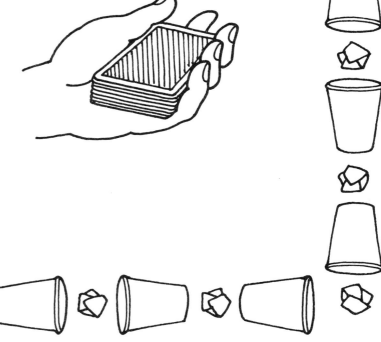

PATTER AND SECRET:

❝ I once met a magician called Loringo. He could see with his fingers. You may not believe me, but I'll try to show you what I mean. First, please shuffle these cards for us. ❞

(Hand cards to somebody to shuffle.)

❝ Thank you very much. May I have the cards now? ❞

(Take back the deck. Hold it up with backs toward the audience, so that you can see the bottom card. Let's say it's the Three of Clubs.)

❝ You've shuffled the deck so the cards are all mixed up. Now I'm going to hold the deck behind me. ❞

(Put the deck behind your back. Be sure you keep track of the bottom card, the Three of Clubs.)

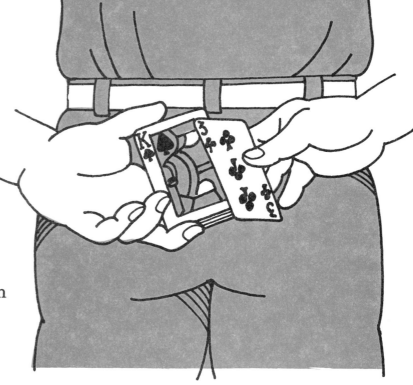

❝ I am now feeling the bottom card. I'm trying to see it with my fingers. ❞

(Flip the Three of Clubs over onto the top of the deck, face up.)

28

3 OF CLUBS

❝The card is—the Three of Clubs.❞

(**Hold the deck up in front of you so the audience can see the Three of Clubs. At the same time, look at the next card. Let's say it's the King of Spades.**)

❝Is that right? The Three of Clubs? Good. But it keeps getting harder.❞

(**Put the deck behind your back. Flip the King of Spades over on top of the Three of Clubs. Hold the deck up in front again, showing the king.**)

❝The King of—let's see—Spades. I told you, it keeps getting harder.❞

(**You can do this as many times as you want. Make a big thing out of feeling the card.**)

❝And that's the greatest trick of the greatest magician in Mule Shoe, Rhode Island. Let's have a big hand for—Loringo!❞

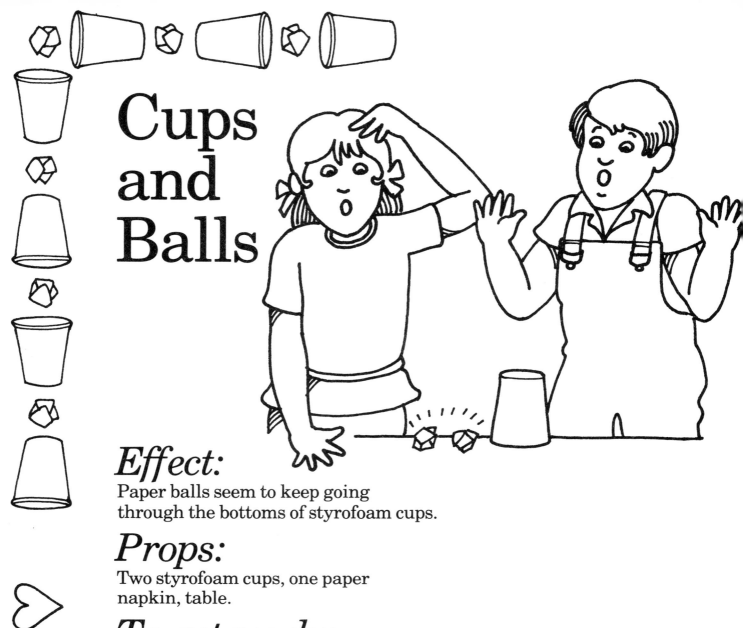

Cups
and
Balls

Effect:

Paper balls seem to keep going
through the bottoms of styrofoam cups.

Props:

Two styrofoam cups, one paper
napkin, table.

To get ready:

Tear the napkin in half. Tear
each half in half again. Roll each piece so that
you have four paper balls. Put the two cups next
to each other, right-side up.
Put one ball into the first cup.
Put the other three balls on
the table to the side of the cups.
Now you're ready.

PATTER AND SECRET:

❝I'm having a problem with these cups and balls. Look. **❞**

(Turn the first cup over. The ball won't fall out. No one will see the ball on the table under the cup. Try it.)

❝I put a ball on top of this cup. Then I put the other cup over the top. If I tap the cup on top, just once, the ball goes right through. **❞**

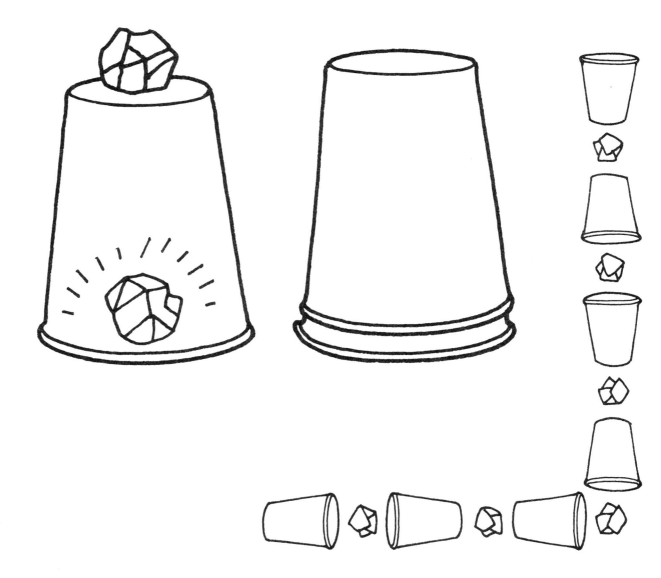

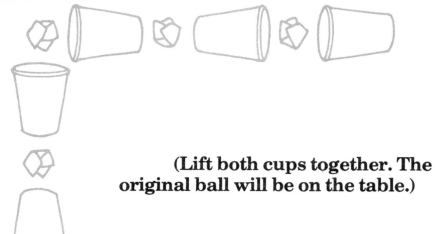

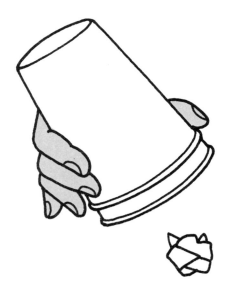

(Lift both cups together. The original ball will be on the table.)

❝ Well, I know what to do. I'll just cover this ball with a cup . . . ❞

(Take the two cups apart. Put the cup that has a ball in it over the ball on the table.)

❝ . . . and put another ball on top, and cover it with the other cup. Now I'll tap the top twice and lift up. Oh, no! It happened again! Well, let's try once more. **❞**

(Put the cup with the ball over the two balls on the table. Put the last ball on the top. Cover it with the other cup.)

❝ Now, this last time I'll tap it three times. **❞**

(Lift up the cups showing three balls on the table.)

❝ I was afraid of that. Well, I'm just going to put these three balls away before they get into any more trouble. Thank you. **❞**

(Drop the three balls into the cup, as shown, and take your bow.)

Wandering Water

Effect:

A cup of water travels from
a popped paper bag back to a hat.

Props:

Two paper cups (same kind),
paper bag, hat, pitcher of water, table.

To get ready:

Cut the bottom out of one of
the cups. Cut the rim off the other cup.
Put the cup without a bottom inside
the other cup. Put the double cup, the hat, the
pitcher of water, and the paper bag
on the table. The bag is folded flat.
Now you're ready.

PATTER AND SECRET:

❝ Water is funny, sometimes. Look, I'll pour some into this cup. Now I'll put the cup into the hat. It'll be all right there for awhile. Let me show you this paper bag. It's not too big, it's not too small. It's just right. Look.**❞**

(Open bag and hold it like this. Reach into hat and very slowly lift out the inside cup, the one that has no bottom. Pretend it has water in it.)

❝ Let's put the cup of water into the bag. **❞**

(Be careful not to show the bottom. Slowly put it into the bag.)

❝ Now, very carefully, we'll close the top of the bag. Watch! **❞**

(Hold the top of the bag tightly with one hand. With the other hand hit the bottom. Bag should break with a BANG! Crumple up the bag and throw it away.)

❝ No, the cup of water isn't gone. Look! **❞**

(Reach into the hat and lift out the cup of water.)

❝ It just likes to wander around. That's what I mean. Water is funny, sometimes. **❞** Thank you.

(Bow.)

Sam the Butter Knife

Effect:

You name the card in the deck where you push in a butter knife.

Props:

Butter knife. (Be sure it has a rounded end, is not sharp, and is very shiny.
Check with Mom, Dad, or your teacher before you do this trick.
Make sure it is a **blunt** knife.)
Deck of cards.

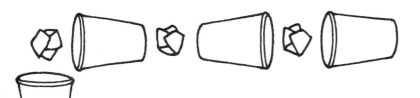

PATTER AND SECRET:

" I would like to show you my friend, Sam. I know he looks like a butter knife, but he's always changing himself into something or other. Right now Sam is a great magician. Look what he can do with a deck of cards. Will you, sir (or madam), please shuffle this deck for Sam? Just mix them up a little. **"**

(After the shuffle, take the deck in your left hand and hold it like this:)

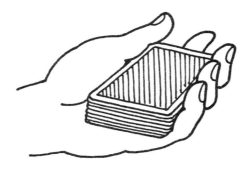

" Now I'll push Sam into the deck so he can look around. **"**

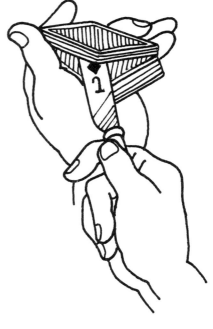

(Push the knife into the deck, then slide it to the left. Tilt the deck to the right a little bit with your left hand. You will be able to see the card corner right above the knife by looking at Sam. Sam becomes a mirror.)

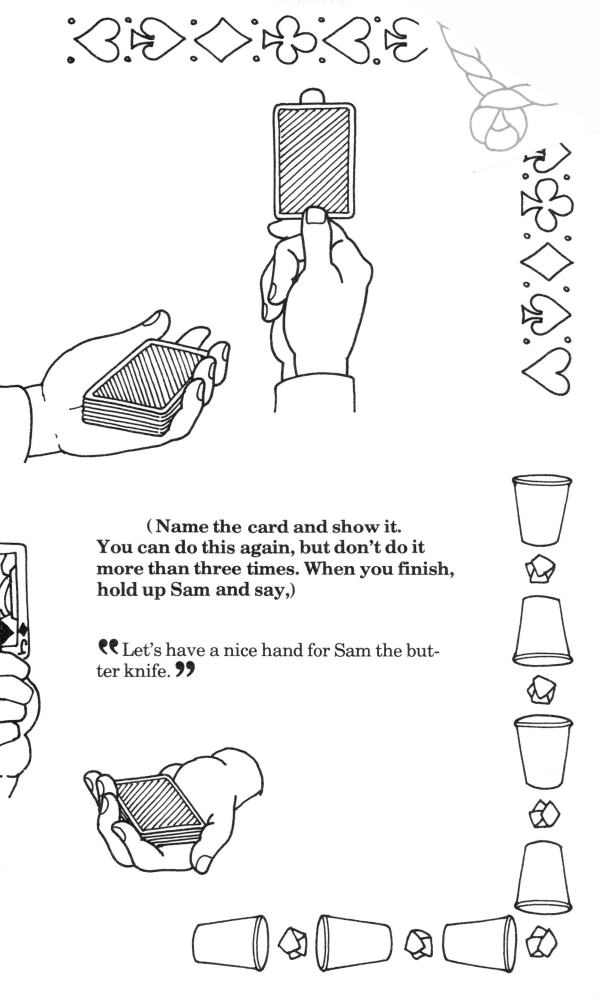

(Name the card and show it.
You can do this again, but don't do it
more than three times. When you finish,
hold up Sam and say,)

❝Let's have a nice hand for Sam the butter knife. ❞

Woofle Rope

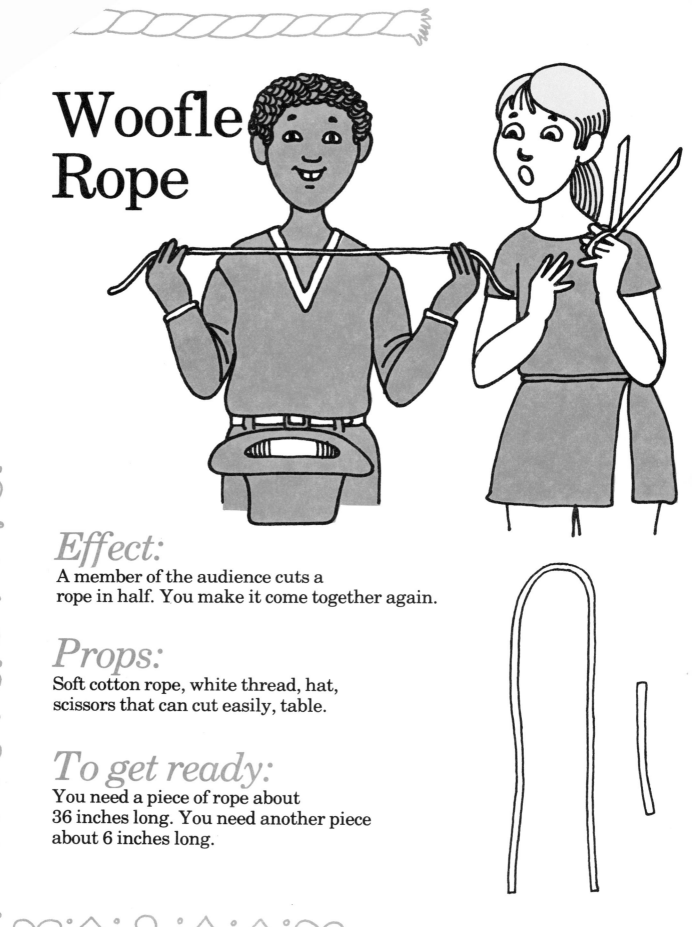

Effect:

A member of the audience cuts a
rope in half. You make it come together again.

Props:

Soft cotton rope, white thread, hat,
scissors that can cut easily, table.

To get ready:

You need a piece of rope about
36 inches long. You need another piece
about 6 inches long.

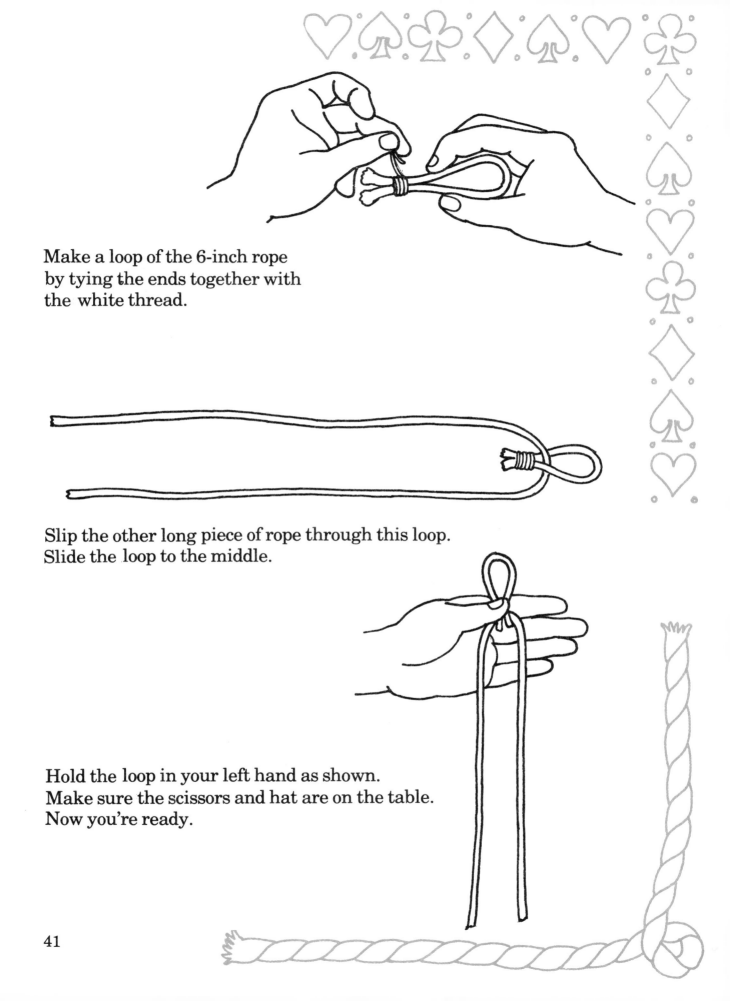

Make a loop of the 6-inch rope
by tying the ends together with
the white thread.

Slip the other long piece of rope through this loop.
Slide the loop to the middle.

Hold the loop in your left hand as shown.
Make sure the scissors and hat are on the table.
Now you're ready.

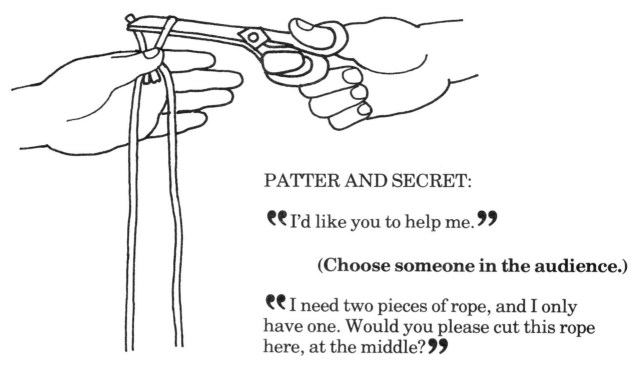

PATTER AND SECRET:

" I'd like you to help me. **"**

(Choose someone in the audience.)

" I need two pieces of rope, and I only have one. Would you please cut this rope here, at the middle? **"**

(You now have what looks like two pieces of rope.)

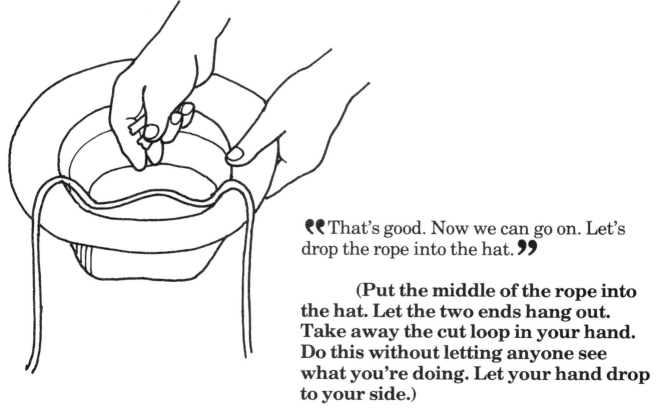

" That's good. Now we can go on. Let's drop the rope into the hat. **"**

(Put the middle of the rope into the hat. Let the two ends hang out. Take away the cut loop in your hand. Do this without letting anyone see what you're doing. Let your hand drop to your side.)

" Does anyone have any woofle dust? No? Well, I think I brought some. **"**

(Put your hand into your pocket and leave the loop there. Pretend to take out some woofle dust.)

" This is what I wanted to do. I wanted to test the woofle dust. I'll sprinkle some over the hat. Now, will you two each hold one of these ropes? **"**

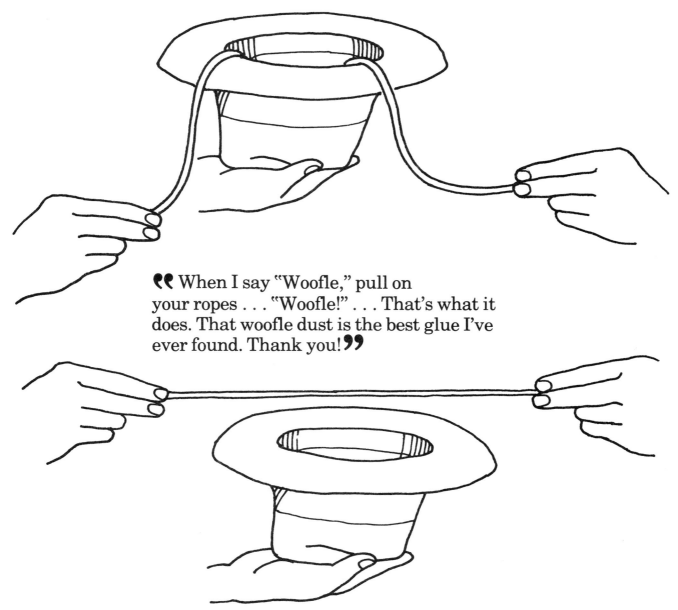

" When I say "Woofle," pull on your ropes . . . . "Woofle!" . . . That's what it does. That woofle dust is the best glue I've ever found. Thank you! **"**

The Card Clock

Effect:

You write down ahead of time the name of the card that the person will choose.

Props:

Deck of cards (take out the jokers)
Pencil
Piece of paper
Table

To get ready:

Count down and find out which card is number 13 from the top of the deck. Let's pretend it's the Nine of Diamonds. Put the deck on the table, face down, next to the paper and pencil. Now you're ready.

PATTER AND SECRET:

❝ Would you please come up here and help me? ❞

(Pick someone in the audience.)

❝ Before we do anything else, I'd like to write you a message. ❞

(Without letting anybody see what you are writing, write the name of the 13th card on the piece of paper—we're pretending it's the Nine of Diamonds. Fold up the piece of paper and hand it to the spectator or place it on the table to the side.)

❝ Please don't look at my message yet. Now, I want you to think of an hour like one o'clock or two o'clock, or any hour. Please don't tell me the hour you are thinking of. I'm going to turn my back now. When I do, I want you to take the same number of cards from the top of the deck as the hour you thought of. For instance, if you thought of two o'clock, take two cards off of the top of the deck. ❞

(Turn around so your back is to the audience.)

❝ Have you taken your cards? Now put them in your pocket or someplace where I can't see them. ❞

(When the spectator is finished doing that, turn back around and face the audience.)

❝Keep thinking of the hour you thought of. Picture a big clock in your mind and see your hour. Here, I'll help you. I'll make a clock of cards. A card clock. For this, I'll need 12 cards.❞

(Deal off 12 cards in a pile, face down, one on top of the other.)

(Pick up the pile, take off the top card and put it face up on the table. That's going to be one o'clock. Keep doing this until you have a card clock that looks like this.)

❝ Now this is very important. Look at this card clock. Look at the hour you thought of. Look at the card that is at that hour. Get a picture of that card in your mind. Do you have that picture? Good. Then I think we're ready. I'm going to tell you three things. First, the hour you thought of was four o'clock. ❞

(You know this because the Nine of Diamonds landed at four o'clock.)

❝ Second, you have four cards in your pocket. ❞

(Ask the spectator to take out the cards and count them. Of course, there will be as many as the hour he or she thought of.)

❝ Third, open the message I wrote to you when we started. What does it say? ❞

(Let spectator read it.)

❝ Nine of Diamonds. Was that your card? ❞

(It has to be because it is the card at four o'clock.)

❝ That's your card, the card at four o'clock, the hour you thought of! Thank you! Now let's have a big hand for all of us and for the clock of cards. ❞

(This trick even fools magicians. But it works itself. Try it!)

Loopy Loop

Effect:

A loop of string seems
to go through a spectator's finger.

Prop:

String (or rope) about
30 to 36 inches long.

PATTER AND SECRET:

❝Here is a string. It's going to play the part of "string." Now I need a finger. It's all right if the finger is attached to a person. Will you please play a part in this story?❞

(Talk to someone's finger.)

❝Guess which part you are going to play! You're going to play the part of "finger." Will you please stand straight up? Now, here is the story. String got itself looped around finger . . .❞

(Put the loop around the finger. Hold the ends of the string with one hand.)

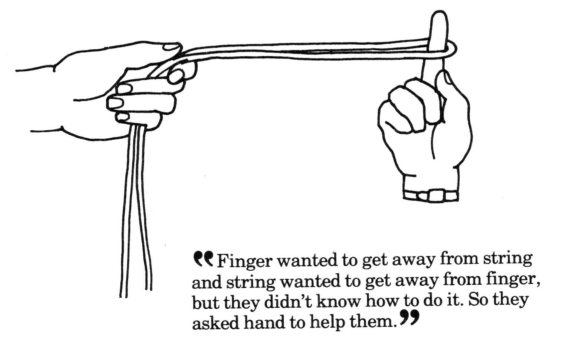

❝Finger wanted to get away from string and string wanted to get away from finger, but they didn't know how to do it. So they asked hand to help them.❞

(Hold up your other hand.)

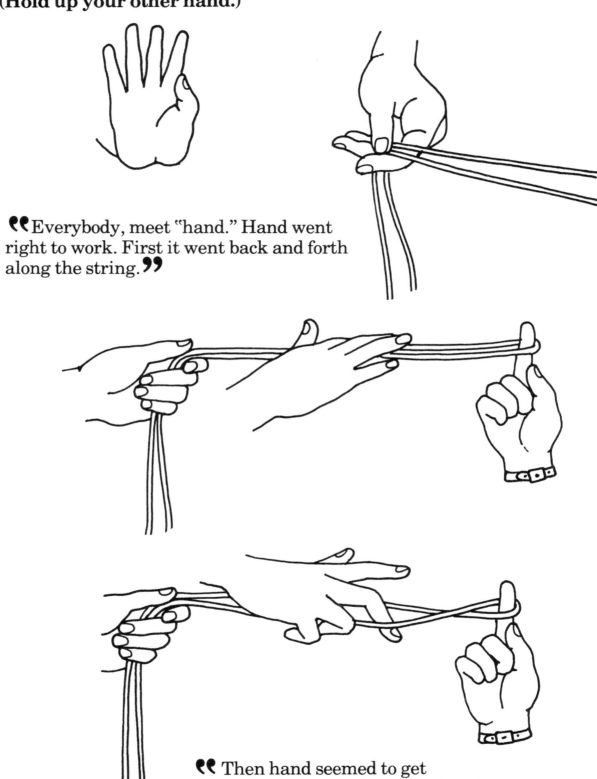

❝Everybody, meet "hand." Hand went right to work. First it went back and forth along the string.**❞**

❝ Then hand seemed to get more tangled up with string than finger already was.**❞**

50

(Look at the pictures and practice what hand does. Make sure you look at the pictures very carefully and do this trick step by step. Practice a lot before you do this in front of an audience. Get a friend to loan a finger.)

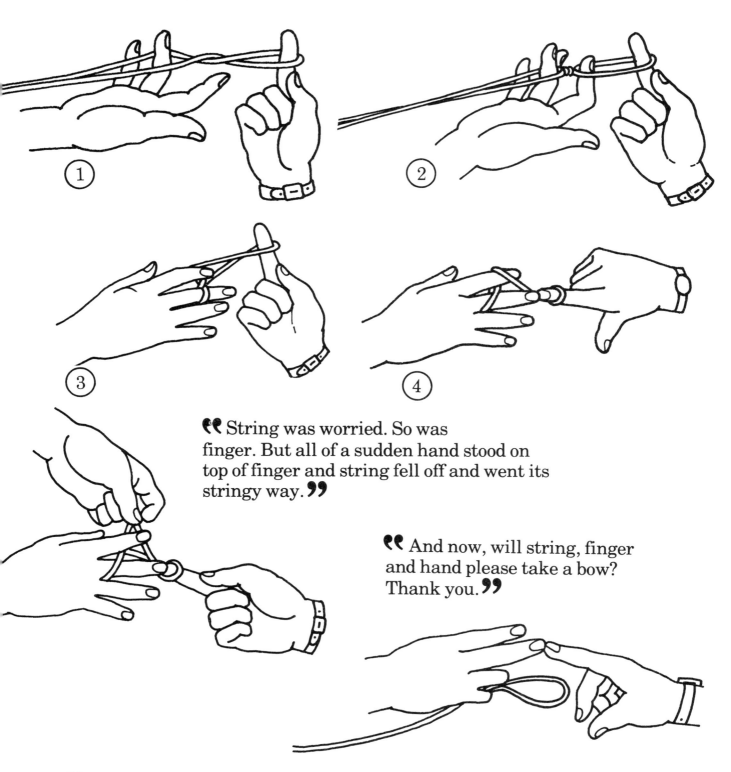

❝ String was worried. So was finger. But all of a sudden hand stood on top of finger and string fell off and went its stringy way. ❞

❝ And now, will string, finger and hand please take a bow? Thank you. ❞

Aces Go Places

Effect:

The 4 aces magically come to the top of 4 piles of cards.

Props:

Deck of cards
Table

To get ready:

Find the 4 aces and put them on top of the deck.

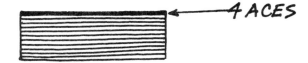

4 ACES

PATTER AND SECRET:

“Please cut the deck in half.**”**

(Ask someone in the audience.)

“Cut it as nearly in half as you can. Now please cut each half in half, as nearly in half as you can.**”**

(Be sure you know which pile has the 4 aces on top of it. This is the pile we'll use last. It will usually wind up being the pile at one end.)

“Please pick up this pile.**”**

(Point to one of the piles that does not have the aces on top.)

“Take three cards off the top of that pile and put them on the bottom. Then put one card from the top of your pile on each of the other 3 piles. Pick up the next pile, please.**”**

(Point to another pile that doesn't have the aces on top.)

❝ Do the same thing. Put 3 cards from the top on the bottom. Then put one card on the tops of the other 3 piles. ❞

(Ask the spectator to do the same thing with the next pile. Point to the 3rd one without the aces.)

❝ Now do the same with this last pile. ❞

(This last time you point to the pile that has the 4 aces.)

❝ Put 3 cards on the bottom and then one card on each of the other 3 piles. Now, these cards are all mixed up. But tell me, what are the most important cards in the deck? Let's see. Please turn over the top card of each pile. Those aces, they really go places! ❞

(This trick works itself. If you want to see how, practice with the aces turned face up and you'll see where they go!)

Grandmother's Necklace

Effect:

Handkerchiefs and rings magically fall off Grandmother's necklace.

Props:

2 ropes
2 handkerchiefs
2 rings
1 pencil
1 hat (any kind)
(Borrow as many of these things
as you can from members of the audience)

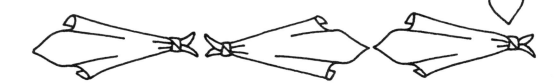

PATTER AND SECRET:

“Grandmother was odd. She wore funny hats.**”**

(Put on hat.)

“She made a necklace out of two ropes.
She started by hanging them over a pencil.**”**

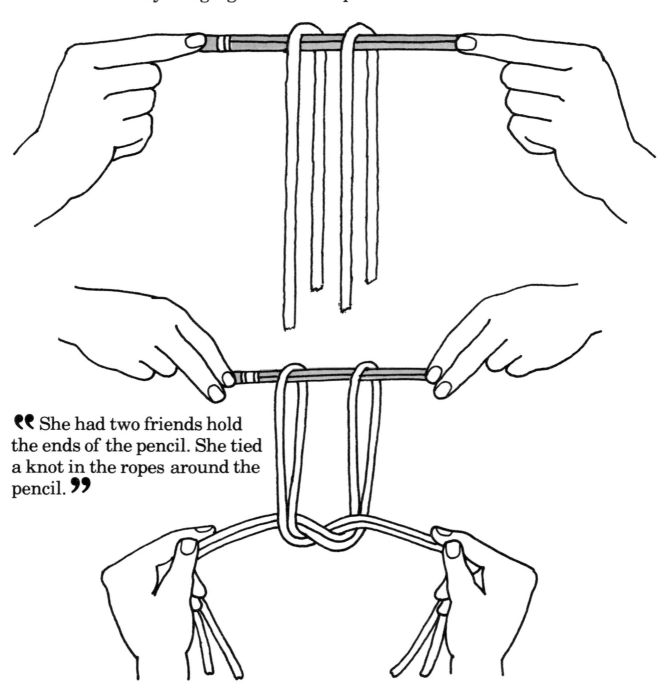

“ She had two friends hold
the ends of the pencil. She tied
a knot in the ropes around the
pencil.**”**

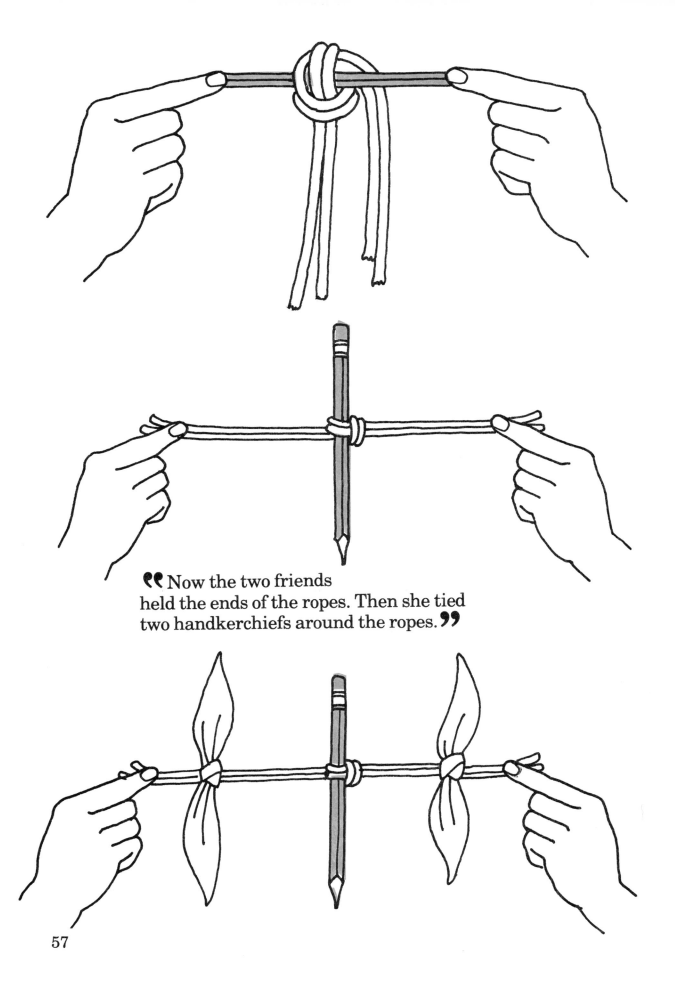

❝Now the two friends
held the ends of the ropes. Then she tied
two handkerchiefs around the ropes.❞

" For a while she wore the necklace like this. Then she slipped two rings onto the ropes next to the handkerchiefs. For a while, she wore the necklace like this. **"**

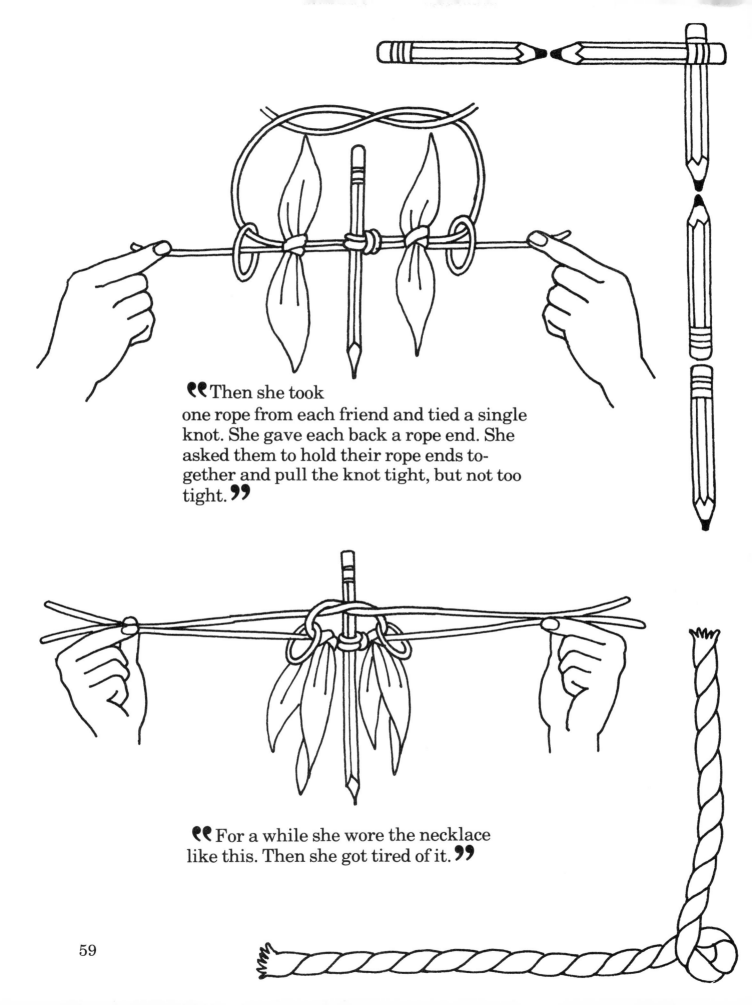

❝Then she took one rope from each friend and tied a single knot. She gave each back a rope end. She asked them to hold their rope ends together and pull the knot tight, but not too tight.**❞**

❝For a while she wore the necklace like this. Then she got tired of it.**❞**

"It was heavy, especially with the two friends hanging on to it. She put the necklace away in her hat. But, she didn't put the two friends in the hat! **"**

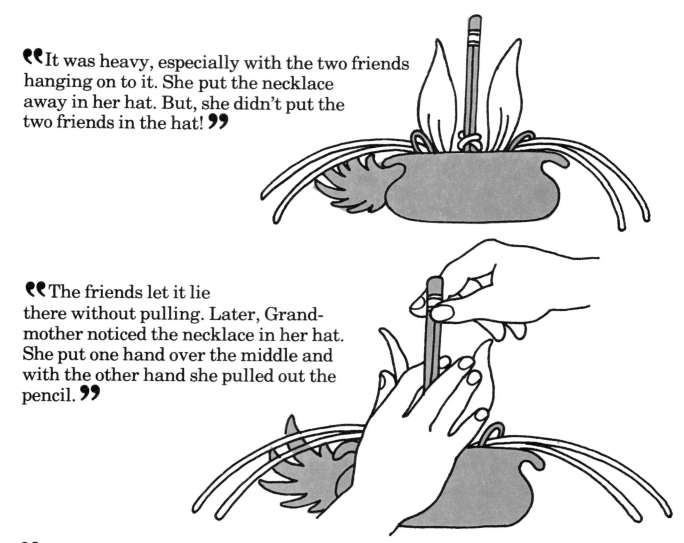

"The friends let it lie there without pulling. Later, Grandmother noticed the necklace in her hat. She put one hand over the middle and with the other hand she pulled out the pencil. **"**

"Then she asked the friends to pull the ropes tight. The handkerchiefs and rings fell off the ropes! Now Grandmother could start all over again. That was Grandmother—she was nice, but she *was* odd! **"**

SECRET:
There is no secret!
This is real magic.
It works itself. Try it!

Backfire

Effect:

You can make a card
amazingly appear in your belt!

Props:

Deck of cards (take out
the jokers—you want to use only
the regular cards), table.

PATTER AND SECRET:

❝Please shuffle these cards for me.❞

(Choose someone from the audience. Help them shuffle if they're not sure how.)

❝Now let me show you that this is just a regular deck.❞

(Hold the deck with the faces of the cards up. Spread the cards from one hand to the other. As you do this, notice which card is at the top of the deck. Let's pretend the top card is the Four of Hearts.)

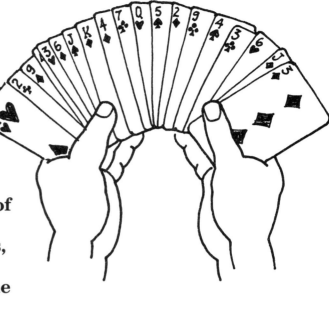

TOP
CARD

❝I am going to leave the cards on the table for you.❞

(Close up deck and put it face down on the table.)

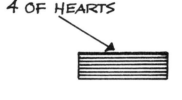

4 OF HEARTS

❝If you'll excuse me, I'll just turn my back for this next part.❞

(Turn around so that your back is to the audience.)

❝Now, please think of a number from 1 to 20. Don't tell me what it is—just think of it.❞

(Let's pretend it's the number 12.)

❝Now take cards from the top of the deck, one at a time, please—just put them down on top of each other next to the deck. Count one for each card, and stop after you get to the number you thought of.❞

(This puts the Four of Hearts on the bottom of the pile of counted cards.)

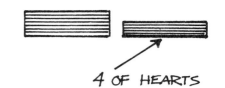

4 OF HEARTS

❝Now look at the next card. Memorize it. Get a picture of that card in your mind. Please put your card back where it was. Now, put the small pile back on top of the deck.❞

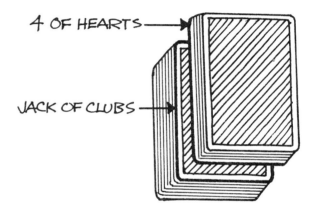

4 OF HEARTS ———→

JACK OF CLUBS ———→

(This puts the Four of Hearts on top of the spectator's card.)

❝Ready?❞

(Turn around when the spectator is ready.)

❝Let me see. You thought of a number which I don't know, and looked at a card which I also don't know. Think very hard about that card.❞

(Pick up the deck, turn the faces toward you, and spread the deck. You can see the spectator's card right next to the Four of Hearts. Here we're pretending that the spectator's card is the Jack of Clubs.)

"Please think harder. Try to send me the picture of your card with your mind. I'll turn around again so I can think better. **"**

(While your back is turned, take out the Jack of Clubs and put it on top of the deck.)

"I think I'm beginning to get the picture. **"**

(Turn around and face front again. Put the deck of cards behind your back. Also have both hands behind your back.)

"I'll tell you what I'm going to do. You keep thinking and I'll try to make the card stick to the wall. **"**

(Take the Jack of Clubs from the top of the deck and put it face out in your belt. As you do this, back up against the wall and pretend to be sticking a card to the wall.)

"There, I think I've got it! **"**

(Move away and look at the wall over your shoulder. Turn. Your back is to the audience. Keep looking at the wall until someone sees it in your belt. Take it out, hold it up and look surprised.)

"Hey! It worked! The picture you sent was perfect. It just backfired, that's all. **"**

(Bow.)